They Followed The Master

Nine Dramas
For Lent

Cynthia S. Baker

CSS Publishing Company, Inc.
Lima, Ohio

THEY FOLLOWED THE MASTER

ISBN 1-55673-704-1   PRINTED IN U.S.A.

To Rev. C. William Cox, and his wife Mary Lou, for their solid friendship, appreciation and warm encouragement, this book is affectionately dedicated.

Table Of
Contents

Introduction

It is my belief that the use of drama in the church adds a lively dimension to the presentation of Bible stories. Jesus, master teacher that he was, used stories constantly to implant truths in his followers' heads. People remembered stories. And stories presented in dramatic form are doubly memorable — you have not only heard the story, you have seen it acted out.

The skits in this book were written for presentation without elaborate scenery, lighting, expensive properties, fancy costumes, or large casts. The parts are short enough so that it is not an overwhelming task to memorize them, although the skits can also be used as reader theater. My intent was to make them easy to put on. I have great sympathy for the small churches, with their limited budgets and humble facilities; I believe they will find this material suitable for their needs.

Production Notes:

The following is a list of cast members by drama.

Lent 1 — Leader (man or woman), Mary

Lent 2 — Leader, John, Andrew

Lent 3 — Leader, Martha, Lazarus

Lent 4 — Leader, Judas, Matthew

Lent 5 — Leader, Joanna

Palm Sunday — Simeon, Jamin, Adah, Timna, Kenaz, Haran, Salma, Perez

Maundy Thursday — Leader, Mother of Judas (Sheerah)

Good Friday — Leader, Cornelius

Easter — Leader, Gabriel, Michael

Cynthia S. Baker

Mary, The Mother Of Jesus

Lent 1

(There are two chairs on a bare stage, set at a conversational distance, turned three quarters toward the congregation, and one quarter toward each other. No scenery is required. Enter LEADER, stage left.)

LEADER: Welcome, everyone, to this service! Tonight will be the first of a series which will introduce you to some of the people who were in some way part of the Lent which preceded the very first Easter. Tonight, we have the privilege of speaking with Mary of Nazareth, wife of Joseph the carpenter, and mother of Jesus. Ma'am, would you join me up here, please?

(MARY, who has been sitting in the front pew, rises and goes up stage right. She is simply dressed in the biblical style, preferably in blue. She is old enough to have a 33-year-old son. She is serene and dignified.)

LEADER: Please be seated. *(MARY sits in one chair; when she is seated, the LEADER sits in the other.)*

LEADER: Now — share with us some of your experiences. We would like to hear what it is like to be the mother of Jesus.

MARY: Where shall I begin? It is a long, long story.

LEADER: Perhaps you can just summarize the earlier days for us, and then bring us up to date. We would like to see the whole picture.

MARY: *(Thinking back, musing.)* What was it like? In the beginning, when the angel Gabriel visited me, it was awesome! He called me "the favored one" when he told me that I, a virgin, would bear a son who would be the Messiah. That was so enormous an idea — I couldn't really grasp it all at once. What did come through, loud and clear, was that I was going to have a baby.

LEADER: And you were engaged at the time, were you not? It must have presented you with some problems!

MARY: You could say that. It meant having to explain the pregnancy to my beloved fiance, when he knew the child could not be his. It meant asking him (and my parents also) to accept as truth a totally incredible story. It meant enduring public shame in small and gossipy Nazareth.

LEADER: But I understand Jesus was not born in Nazareth, but in Bethlehem.

MARY: Yes.

LEADER: Was that a glorious event — the birth of the Son of God?

MARY: Some of the people who came to look at the baby spoke of a special star, or of angels — but for Joseph and me, it was a strange and frightening time, in a stable among the animals. And because we had to flee almost immediately from the wrath of King Herod, there was danger, and exile, and loneliness in those early years, until we could return to Nazareth and settle down to normal living.

LEADER: Did you and Joseph have children?

MARY: Oh yes. We had six, four sons and two daughters. We had many years of quiet happiness. Then Joseph died of a fever, and Jesus took over the carpenter shop. He is a fine carpenter, as Joseph was.

LEADER: But then came the call of Jesus to his public ministry.

MARY: Yes. And that created problems within the family. The other boys thought Jesus had no right to leave the carpenter shop and go wandering around the countryside. If Joseph had lived, it might have been different, but they believed that Jesus as the oldest should stay in the shop.

LEADER: What about you, Mary? What did you think?

MARY: I confess I didn't really understand it, either. This new life that Jesus is leading — how does that fit with what the angel told me, about his being the Messiah, and sitting on the throne of David? And he is making enemies left and right. Jesus is a marvelous teacher, of course, and I can understand why the throngs of people crowd around him and follow him; and they say he also does miracles of healing. But in every crowd there are spies from the temple — priests and Pharisees — and they are always angry with him. They are powerful people! Their anger is dangerous!

LEADER: So you are worried about Jesus' safety.

MARY: I don't want to call it worry. When one has faith in God, it is wrong to worry. But I am very much aware that he is in danger.

When Jesus was little, I was sure he was protected by whole squadrons of angels. All through the terrible danger from

Herod — all through the trip to Egypt, and the lonely years away from home, all through his childhood in Nazareth, the angels seemed to be there. His every step seemed to be guarded.

LEADER: And now?

MARY: *(With growing distress)* Now I pray daily for his safety and the only answer I seem to hear from God is an echo of the prophecy we heard so long ago from old Simeon in the temple, when Jesus was dedicated. He said to us, "Behold, he is destined to cause the falling and rising of many in Israel, and to be a sign that is spoken against; and a sword will pierce through your own soul also ..." That's what he said — speaking to me! A sword will pierce my soul also. Does that mean that first a sword will pierce the soul of Jesus? I am so afraid for him! What does it all mean? *(She hides her face in her hands.)*

LEADER: *(Getting to his feet)* I am afraid we have upset you, Mary. I am sorry.

MARY: *(She also rises)* It's all right. My concern for Jesus is always with me — my wonderful, very special son. I will be going to Jerusalem for the Passover soon, with my family; and I feel certain that Jesus and his disciples will be there, too. Something is going to happen — I feel it, I know it! I wish I knew what it is! But whatever happens, I want to be there. And God will be with me.

LEADER: I'm sure he will. Thank you for talking with us, Mary.

MARY: Goodbye.

Exit, stage right. LEADER stands looking after her; then exits, stage left.)

John And Andrew

Lent 2

(There are two chairs on stage. Enter LEADER, stage left.)

LEADER: One striking thing in the narratives about Jesus, just before his last trip to Jerusalem, is the fact that he told his disciples, not once but three times, that he would be delivered up to his enemies and put to death.

No conversations among his disciples have been recorded about this, but it would seem inevitable that they must have discussed this strange and ominous prophecy among themselves. Let us listen in to two disciples, and a conversation that MIGHT have taken place.)

(Exit LEADER, stage right.)

(Enter ANDREW and JOHN, apparently in the middle of a conversation.)

ANDREW: *(agitated)* I tell you, John, I don't understand it at all. Do you realize that three times now, three times, Jesus has told us that he will be delivered to his enemies, and mocked, and scourged, and crucified? Just how does that fit with Jesus, the Messiah?

13

(The two men sit down in the two chairs, turned one quarter toward each other, and three quarters toward the congregation.)

JOHN: I'm beginning to think we haven't understood the Master's mission right along.

ANDREW: Meaning what?

JOHN: Andrew, you and I go back a long ways.

ANDREW: A very long ways. I can't remember a time when we were not friends.

JOHN: But you and I were disciples, even before my brother James and your brother Peter were disciples. Do you remember? We were followers of the prophet John, the one they called the Baptizer.

ANDREW: That's right, we were. Right up until the day he pointed out Jesus to me.

JOHN: Do you remember what John called him that day?

ANDREW: Of course — he said, "Behold, the Lamb of God, who takes away the sin of the world."

JOHN: All right, hold on to that thought for a minute. Now, remember, back to the time when Jesus fed the 5,000 people on a few loaves and fishes. Do you remember what Jesus said about himself that day?

ANDREW: *(sounding puzzled)* Yes — he called himself the bread of life, the bread that came down from heaven.

JOHN: Right. And do you remember the day he healed the man born blind — what did Jesus call himself that day?

ANDREW: He called himself the light of the world. What on earth are you driving at, John?

JOHN: Those titles — the bread of life, the light of the world — were associated with events — with things that actually happened to demonstrate the titles. But what about the title John the Baptizer gave him — the Lamb of God, who takes away the sin of the world. Think, Andrew, think! Think about the temple at Jerusalem, where we're headed. What happens to lambs in the temple?

ANDREW: *(With growing horror, as he realizes the direction the conversation is taking)* They sacrifice them for sin — John, you aren't saying you think he's just going to walk up and let them kill him — you can't mean that!

JOHN: I don't really know what I mean! But you and I both know he is the Son of God, and we've seen the kind of power he has. I don't believe any enemy can hurt him — unless he lets them. Yet that's what he's told us — three times, now — that his enemies will put him to death. I'm afraid for him, Andrew! The Lamb of God!

ANDREW: But the scriptures say that the Messiah will sit on the throne of David, and reign forever. How does that fit with a sacrificial Lamb?

JOHN: I don't know. But the prophet Isaiah also talks about a suffering Messiah, wounded for our transgressions, and bruised for our iniquities, led like a lamb to the slaughter, to die for our sins.

ANDREW: I'm not familiar with that part of the prophecy.

JOHN: The priests don't read it much, because as you say, it doesn't seem to fit with the triumphant Messiah who's going to sit on the throne. And I don't know how it fits, either. I only know that both pictures of the Messiah must be right. God's word is truth.

15

ANDREW: But if what you're suggesting is true, then he's going to his death — and we're going with him! What can we do, John?

JOHN: I don't think there's anything we can do. You heard what he said to Peter, when Peter tried to dissuade him. Jesus is our Master. We are followers, not advisors.

ANDREW: *(heavily)* That's right — followers. Where he goes, we go. But God help us all!

(Exeunt, stage right.)

Martha And Lazarus

Lent 3

(There is a small table on stage, with two chairs. Enter LEADER, stage left.)

LEADER: Perhaps the most spectacular healing miracle that Jesus performed was the restoring of life to his friend Lazarus, after the man had been dead and buried for four days. The account is given in John's gospel, chapter 11, verses 1-44.

(OPTIONAL: Scripture can be read here, if desired.)

LEADER: The events of the following skit represent something that might have happened, in the days following the miracle. Let us listen to an imagined conversation between MARTHA and her healed brother LAZARUS.

(Exit LEADER, stage left. Enter MARTHA, stage left, carrying a clothes basket with something she can be folding as she talks — pillowcases or napkins are good. She looks down the aisle as if looking for someone; then sets the basket on the table, and, still standing, begins folding the contents carefully, making a pile of the folded items on the table beside her. It is obvious that she is taking pains to fold them exactly.)

(Enter LAZARUS, stage right.)

17

MARTHA: *(sounding relieved)* Well, here you are — finally!

LAZARUS: *(Seating himself in one of the chairs, which he pulls away from the table so as not to interfere with what MARTHA is doing.)* Mary says you've been fretting all the time I've been gone. What's the matter, Martha? Anyone would think I've never been to Jerusalem by myself before!

MARTHA: First, look out that window, and tell me if that fat priest is still across the street, watching the house.

LAZARUS: *(Standing up and walking over to front stage right, looking out over the congregation as if looking through a window.)* A priest, you say? There was somebody there when I arrived home, but he isn't there now. You think someone is spying on us?

MARTHA: I don't just think it — I know it.

LAZARUS: *(seating himself again)* What on earth for? Because we're friends of Jesus, you think?

MARTHA: That, and more. Lazarus, ever since Jesus raised you from death to life, more and more people have begun to believe in him as the Messiah. The streams of people coming into Bethany are three times the normal traffic — and they all visit the tomb where you were buried.

LAZARUS: But that's all to the good, isn't it? Wouldn't Jesus be pleased? Isn't that what his mission is all about — to persuade people he is the Son of God, with power even over death?

MARTHA: *(Speaking very earnestly — she has stopped folding things)* Of course it's good, in that sense. But the Pharisees and priests are not pleased. The word on the street is that they are plotting to kill Jesus — and what is more, they're plotting to kill you, too, because the miracle Jesus performed on you is something they can't explain away.

LAZARUS: They wouldn't dare touch Jesus! The crowds would tear them to pieces! They hang on his every word!

MARTHA: Oh, they won't do it when the crowds are there. *(She draws out the other chair, and sits down near Lazarus.)* But the crowds go home at night. And it's at night that Jesus is vulnerable. And so are you. What protection do we have? Only a few servants. Jesus and his disciples are planning to be with us during the Passover celebration. I am afraid the priests may make some kind of move then.

LAZARUS: Calm yourself, Martha. You are such a worrier! Jesus has handled the priests and Pharisees before, in a masterful way. He has been threatened with arrest many times, and always he has escaped their clutches.

MARTHA: *(doubtfully)* I suppose you're right — he can handle himself. He is the Son of God, after all. But what about you, Lazarus? They are planning to put you to death, too!

LAZARUS: Well, if it will make you feel better, I can spread the word around here in Bethany. We have many friends; we could raise a mob in Bethany at a moment's notice — one the priests would find very difficult to deal with, for they have no legitimate charges against me, as everybody here knows.

MARTHA: That would make me feel better. There is a lot of protection in a big crowd of people. Even the soldiers of Pilate think twice before coming to grips with a Jewish mob! And it would also make me feel better if you would be more careful about exposing yourself to danger.

LAZARUS: I can't hide in the house, Martha. I am a follower of the Master — I don't want to miss anything that happens in Jerusalem while he's there.

MARTHA: *(agitated)* But Mary and I are just getting used to having you back again! You don't know how hard it was for us, when you died! We don't want to lose you again!

LAZARUS: *(He stands up and pats Martha's shoulder)* I can appreciate your feelings, Martha. But you must understand — the life I am living now, that Jesus gave me, belongs to him. I am sorry if you feel I am endangering myself needlessly, but we three, you and I and Mary, may well be the best friends he has except for his band of disciples. And we must be willing to serve him in any way we can, no matter what it costs us. Isn't that right?

MARTHA: *(brokenly)* You are right, of course. *(Pulling herself together)* And I am planning to serve him. He promised to visit us six days before the Passover, and we will prepare a wonderful feast and welcome for him! *(She stands up)*

LAZARUS: That's the spirit! I knew I could count on you! And we can count on Mary, too.

(Martha picks up her pile of folded things, lays them on top of her basket, and picks up the basket.)

LAZARUS: Here — let me carry that for you. *(He takes the basket.)* Is dinner almost ready?

MARTHA: Dinner — ! Why of course! Mercy! You must be starved. I'll see about it at once.

(Exit MARTHA, hurriedly, followed by LAZARUS with the basket, stage right.)

Judas
And
Matthew

Lent 4

(Scene opens with MATTHEW, seated center stage at a small table, writing on a tablet. There is another chair, stage left. Enter LEADER, stage left.)

LEADER: As Jesus entered the last few weeks of his life, the animosity of his enemies grew with every miracle he performed, every teaching he gave. In the little band of disciples, there must have been tension and uneasiness. In particular, one wonders how it happened that one of the faithful 12 turned on his master, and betrayed him. Let us listen to an imaginary conversation that the disciple Judas might have had with the disciple Matthew.

(Exit LEADER, stage right. Enter JUDAS, stage left.)

JUDAS: Matthew, can I talk to you?

MATTHEW: *(looking up, pen in hand)* Sure, Judas — what's on your mind?

(JUDAS picks up chair, stage left, and brings it over to Matthew's table. Matthew puts down his pen, and pushes the tablet of paper to one side.)

21

JUDAS: Things are going all wrong!

MATTHEW: What do you mean?

JUDAS: You remember how, when we came into the city, the crowd was shouting their support all around us, and Jesus was riding on the donkey, and people were throwing palm branches in front of him and calling him the Son of David?

MATTHEW: Of course! It was wonderful! You have a problem with that?

JUDAS: No, no — It was what happened after that. It's all very well to have the support of the people — naturally, we want that — but surely, Jesus can't believe that he can ever become a king without the support of the really important people, the Pharisees, the Sadducees, the priests — yet every move he makes antagonizes them!

MATTHEW: You mean his throwing the money changers out of the temple?

JUDAS: Among other things — yes! Come on, Matthew! Money changers are legitimate businessmen! You used to work for the Romans as a tax official — you understand business! Jesus knocked over all those tables, and scattered money all over the floor, and released all those pigeons and lambs — what a mess it was! And the temple authorities were furious!

MATTHEW: You heard what the Master said. The money changers were cheats and robbers in a house of prayer.

(JUDAS pushes back his chair and begins to pace up and down.)

JUDAS: Yes, well — I suppose there are some abuses that need to be cleaned up. But there are other ways to accomplish things!

You have to cooperate with people who are in power! You have to compromise! Jesus is placing himself — and all the rest of us — in great danger!

MATTHEW: Jesus doesn't compromise. He feels very strongly about the sacredness of the temple.

JUDAS: And what on earth did he hope to accomplish with that denunciation of the Pharisees yesterday — calling them blind guides and hypocrites, and whitewashed tombs full of dead bones, for crying out loud! He's made enemies left and right. They wouldn't support him now if he called down a whole sky full of angels!

MATTHEW: Judas, are you trying to say Jesus doesn't know what he's doing?

JUDAS: Yes! I mean, no! I mean — is he going to turn everything upside down? *(pleading)* Matthew, I thought surely you would understand what I'm saying. These things he's doing — this is not the way!

MATTHEW: Calm down, Judas. I understand, all right. I think all of us are uneasy. And we know there's danger. But I believe Jesus is the Messiah, and I don't intend to tell him what to do, or not to do.

JUDAS: But somebody should at least suggest he soften his approach — he's risking everything!

MATTHEW: Don't you remember when Peter tried to tell him not to come to Jerusalem because it would be dangerous? And Jesus turned on him, shouting, "Get thee behind me, Satan?" No sir — I'm not going to do it. I'm going to follow him, and take what comes. How about you? Are you with us, or not?

JUDAS: *(hastily)* Of course. I never said I wasn't. I'm just concerned, that's all. No law against that, is there?

MATTHEW: Not if that's all it is.

JUDAS: *(preparing to leave — his manner is changed, falsely hearty)* Well, I won't take up any more of your time. *(He turns away — then turns back)* I say — there won't be any need to tell anyone we had this conversation. Just between us, right?

MATTHEW: You aren't going to do anything stupid, are you, Judas?

JUDAS: Me? No, no. I'm completely loyal to the Master — completely loyal. You know that.

MATTHEW: All right. If you say so. We all have to remember who's in charge.

JUDAS: Who's in charge. Right. See you, Matthew.

(Exit JUDAS, stage left, hastily. MATTHEW looks after him, shrugs, then picks up his pen and paper and exits, stage right.)

Joanna, Wife Of Chuza

Lent 5

(Enter LEADER, stage left)

LEADER: With us tonight is a court lady, from the palace of King Herod, the Lady Joanna.

(Enter JOANNA, stage right, a well-dressed middle-aged lady, wearing a long tunic of expensive fabric, and a himation, a long scarf draped over left shoulder and across body, held in place by sash. She is carrying a folded robe, which she places on a chair.)

JOANNA: My name is Joanna, and I live in two very different worlds. Because my husband, Chuza, is steward to King Herod, I am one of the court ladies. I put in an occasional appearance there, when my husband insists — dressed like this.

(She turns around so that the audience can see her dress.)

But when I can call my time my own, I join the women who provide for the needs of Jesus of Nazareth, and his band of disciples.

(She removes the himation and lays it over the back of the chair; picks up the folded robe which is made of coarser material with sleeves, and puts it on.)

LEADER: That makes quite a transformation! I must confess it is unexpected to find a court lady like yourself waiting on a band of travelling disciples!

JOANNA: Does that surprise you? Perhaps it would make more sense if I told you that about a year ago, I was struck with paralysis on my right side — face, arm, leg. I had a devoted little maid named Rebekah who insisted I be taken on a litter to where Jesus of Nazareth was preaching to the multitudes.

(She walks slowly back and forth on the stage, remembering.)

He was also healing the sick and he healed me that day, not only of the paralysis, but of the bitter spirit that had possessed me. From that day, he has been my Master, my Lord. I have done my best to show gratitude by providing meals and other small services for him and his disciples.

(She heaves a big sigh.)

That's over now, of course.

LEADER: Tell us about the last time you saw Jesus.

JOANNA: I was at court last Friday, when Jesus was brought to Herod by the soldiers of Pilate, the Roman governor. The Jewish religious leaders had always resented Jesus and they had finally arrested, tried, and delivered him to Pilate for execution on charges of blasphemy — to be killed for claiming to be who he really was!

LEADER: Wasn't it rather unusual for Pilate to involve Herod in a court case? It surprises me that Pilate didn't just deal with the situation.

(JOANNA is walking back and forth again.)

JOANNA: I don't think Pilate wanted to make this particular decision. He was hoping Herod would do the job for him, because Jesus was a Galilean, and Herod is Tetrarch of Galilee.

LEADER: What was Herod's reaction?

JOANNA: Herod was really excited to see Jesus, and perhaps apprehensive, too. He is a superstitious man. He said once he thought Jesus must be John the Baptist, come back from the dead to haunt him. Everybody in the palace knew that Herod had terrible nightmares after he had ordered the death of John. (We used to hear him screaming in the night.)

But what excited him about Jesus was that he had heard about miracles Jesus had done. He wanted to see something miraculous done before him — as if Jesus was some kind of magician doing tricks for his entertainment.

Jesus just stood there calmly. Although it was obvious he had been beaten and abused, and his hands were tied, he was the most impressive figure in the room. No matter how hard Herod tried, he couldn't get even one word out of him — to say nothing of a miracle.

LEADER: A stand-off, you might say. What happened then?

JOANNA: Herod became angry, and went into one of his famous rages. He had an old purple robe brought out, and had the soldiers drape it over Jesus, saying that if the man thought he was royal, he should be dressed royally. The soldiers abused him, and made fun of him, pretending to kneel in homage.

(Speaking slowly and impressively)

But the strange thing was the effect that the purple robe had on Herod. I was watching his face, and I saw him actually turn pale when he saw Jesus with the purple over his shoulders. Even though Jesus was bound, and his face swollen and bruised, the purple suddenly looked right on him — the kingly color on a man who had every right to wear purple because he was a king, and a king of kings. For just a moment Herod saw it, and there was naked fear in his eyes.

(She pauses for a moment, remembering. Her voice changes.)

The moment passed, of course. When Jesus continued to stand quietly, making no effort to defend himself, Herod's control returned. "Take him back to Pilate," he ordered the soldiers. "He's Pilate's problem, not mine."

LEADER: And they took him away?

JOANNA: They took him away. That was the last time I saw my Master alive. But this I know: someday I shall see him again, and he will be standing in glory, in glorious royal garments, crowned with a glorious royal crown — King of kings, and Lord of lords!

(With a note of triumph in her voice)

And where he is, there I shall be also!

(Exit JOANNA, stage right.)

(Exit LEADER, stage left.)

The Triumphal Entry

Palm Sunday

SCENE: A road outside of Jerusalem. Scenery is not required; the skit can be played against a neutral background.

(Enter SIMEON, stage left, a Pharisee, in a rich-looking robe. He paces back and forth on the stage once or twice, pausing occasionally to look down the center aisle as if expecting someone, and shading his eyes with one hand as if standing in bright sunlight.)

(Enter JAMIN, also a Pharisee, similarly dressed, stage left.)

JAMIN: What do you think, Simeon? Will he come?

SIMEON: *(irritably)* How can anyone tell? We have our spies out, watching the roads. But the city is alive with rumors. It is difficult to sort out the truth.

JAMIN: He would be a fool to come. He must know we're waiting to arrest him.

SIMEON: Oh he knows, all right. But you know how many times we've thought we had him trapped — and he's always managed to elude us. He's as slippery as an eel!

(They both look down the aisle, shading their eyes.)

(ADAH and TIMNA, two humbly dressed women, approach the stage from the right, talking excitedly as they come. They too are looking down the center aisle from time to time. They see the Pharisees, but stay carefully on stage right. The two Pharisees draw back a little toward stage left, as if afraid of contamination. At the same time, however, they appear to be trying to listen in on the women's conversation.)

ADAH: I tell you, Timna, I saw him! They'll be using this road if they're coming to Jerusalem.

TIMNA: Tell me again about the donkey.

ADAH: It was in Bethphage. Jesus sent Peter and John to untie a donkey's colt that was tethered out in the street. At first people who were standing around asked them what they were doing; but they only answered, "The Lord has need of it!" and the people let them go. They brought the colt to Jesus, and he is riding on it.

TIMNA: Maybe he's tired.

ADAH: Tired! I shouldn't wonder if he was! But somehow, I don't think that's it. He's been tired before, but he's never ridden before. And there's something else. That donkey, Timna — it was an unbroken colt, never ridden before — yet, when Jesus mounted it, it was as meek and gentle as a lamb!

SIMEON: *(sternly, stepping forward)* Woman, did you say Jesus of Nazareth is coming into Jerusalem on a donkey?

TIMNA: *(fearfully)* Don't tell him, Adah!

ADAH: I couldn't say, I'm sure. There was such a crowd.

(While she is speaking, KENAZ and HARAN, two humbly dressed men, drift onto the stage from the right, also looking occasionally down the aisle, and pantomiming a conversation.)

SIMEON: *(angrily)* But you said something about Jesus and a donkey! I demand to know what you said!

(JAMIN steps forward and pulls SIMEON back.)

JAMIN: *(aside)* Not now, Simeon! This is not the place! A crowd is beginning to gather.

(While JAMIN is speaking, SALMA, a middle-aged woman, and PEREZ, an older man, enter, stage right, and join the "crowd.")

SIMEON: *(letting himself be pulled back)* If I had her back at the temple, I'd get the truth out of her! Don't you see, Jamin? If Jesus comes into the city on a donkey, it will be like making an announcement! People will remember that prophecy in the scroll of Zechariah, "Behold, your king comes, humble, and riding on a donkey."

JAMIN: *(urgently)* They will certainly remember it if you remind them!

(The two Pharisees draw together, stage left, glaring at the "crowd." The "crowd" of others is bunched at the right of the stage, chattering in pantomime together, and looking often down the aisle. They are restless, constantly shifting places. KENAZ and HARAN wiggle their way past ADAH and TIMNA to the front.)

KENAZ: Jesus' friends from Bethany are here somewhere. I'd like to see Lazarus. They say Jesus raised him from the dead.

HARAN: Yes — he did! I was there! I tell you, Kenaz, I've seen a lot of things, but when Lazarus, who had been dead for three days — three days, mind you - when he walked out of that grave, I almost fainted. And I wasn't the only one.

(SIMEON has been listening. He steps forward again.)

SIMEON: Here, fellow! Don't go around saying things like that!

HARAN: But I saw it — with my own eyes!

SIMEON: *(angrily)* You were deceived! The man's an imposter!

TIMNA: *(from the crowd)* He's a healer!

JAMIN: He's a blasphemer!

SALMA: *(from the crowd)* He's a teacher!

SIMEON: He's a peasant!

PEREZ: *(from the crowd)* He's a prophet!

JAMIN: He's the son of a carpenter!

HARAN: *(from the crowd)* He's the Son of God!

(There is a moment of shocked silence.)

SIMEON: *(furiously)* Who said that! Blasphemy! Blasphemy!

KENAZ: *(pointing down the aisle)* Look! He's coming! Jesus is coming!

CROWD: Jesus is coming!

HARAN: What are we waiting for? Come on!

(The crowd pours down off the stage, left, practically running over the Pharisees, who are forced to the back. The persons in the crowd are shouting the following speeches as they come, ALL AT THE SAME TIME, each one repeating his line over and over until they are out of sight at the back of the room.)

ADAH: Hosanna! Jesus, Jesus!

TIMNA: Blessed is the King who comes in the name of the Lord!

KENAZ: Blessed be the prophet of Nazareth!

HARAN: Praise to the son of David!

SALMA: Hosanna in the highest!

PEREZ: Hosanna! Hosanna! Jesus, Jesus, Jesus!

(The two Pharisees, brushing themselves off as though the crowd has soiled their robes, come to the front of the stage, looking after the crowd. SIMEON is glaring, and standing with legs apart and hands on hips.)

JAMIN: We can do nothing. Look — the whole world has gone after him!

SIMEON: So it seems. For today, at least. *(He turns to JAMIN and holds one finger up in warning.)* But mark my words, Jamin — it won't last. That crowd is as fickle as weather. Our time will come — and soon!

(Exeunt SIMEON and JAMIN, stage left.)

The Mother Of Judas

Maundy Thursday

(Enter LEADER, stage left)

LEADER: What was it like to be the mother of Judas Iscariot?

The people of the Lenten story did not exist in a vacuum. They all had families, and relationships, and backgrounds, about which we know only a little from the pages of scripture.

But let us imagine what it might have been like. Let us listen to a woman named Sheerah, of Kerioth, whose son was called Judas Iscariot. The word "Iscariot" probably means "from Kerioth," which was about 12 miles south of Hebron. It was a name associated with Judas, simply to distinguish him from other men named Judas, which was a common name in those days. I will see if we can persuade Judas' mother to talk to us.

(LEADER leaves stage, stage left, and goes over to SHEER-AH, who is sitting in first pew on the right. She whispers to her, and after a minute, LEADER sits down in the pew, and SHEERAH comes up, stage right.)

SHEERAH: I've had a hard time deciding if I want to talk to you about my son, or not. A lot of the Christians don't want to have anything to do with me. And it's a painful subject — but it might be a relief to talk, at that. There's a lot bottled up inside me.

(She looks out over the audience, from face to face.)

You look as though some of you must be mothers. Maybe even mothers with grown children. Well — have all your children turned out just the way you wanted them to? Well, have they?

My husband Jotham and I had such high hopes for Judas. We had six boys, but Judas was the smart one. *(proudly)* He learned so fast how to read, and especially he was quick with numbers. When he was just a boy, Jotham would let him keep the books at our pottery shop, and sometimes he waited on customers. We were proud of the way he handled money. And he could drive a sharp bargain with the best of them!

We had hopes of his becoming a scribe, perhaps a temple scribe — he was certainly smart enough, and ambitious enough, too. But what Judas himself seemed to want was money, and the care of money. Lots of money. He was enthusiastic about helping Jotham in the shop, but he was more interested in making a big profit than in providing a quality product. Jotham was dedicated to making his pots the very best; Judas wanted them to bring the very best prices.

It seemed to be an obsession with him, and I worried about it sometimes, I can remember wondering if there was anything Judas wouldn't be willing to do — for money. I kept my thoughts to myself, because Jotham was so proud of him — but to me it was like seeing a dark streak in a piece of white marble.

(She walks across the stage, and comes back.)

But then Jesus of Nazareth came along. Crowds of people, especially young people, flocked to hear this young Rabbi teach, and to see the miracles that began to happen almost everywhere he went. Judas came home, I remember, fired with excitement, because Jesus had chosen him to be a disciple. He, Judas from Kerioth, had been singled out for this honor — the only disciple who was not from Galilee!

And I have to say — at first, I was glad. I thought it would do him good. I hoped association with Jesus might tame Judas' wild craving for money. I even convinced myself — fool that I was! — that perhaps Judas could be of help to Jesus, to see that his ministry was properly funded.

He passed his hat through the crowds, you know, to take up offerings while Jesus was teaching, or healing. He even told me that Jesus had entrusted him with the moneybag. I hoped he wasn't dipping into it for himself, as he used to do with his father's moneybox. Jotham never knew, but I did.

But things didn't get better — they got worse. Judas got it into his head that this Jesus could even be the Messiah — that maybe the people would demand he be made a king! And Judas, of course, saw the opportunity to rise to the top like cream in a bottle; he wanted to be treasurer, or minister of finance, or some such thing, when Jesus became king.

Unfortunately for Judas, Jesus wasn't a bit interested. He had a mission, but it wasn't to be king. He antagonized many of the temple leaders when Judas thought he should be trying to cooperate with them. He let some woman anoint his feet with nard that was worth a year's wages — Judas was appalled at what he saw as terrible waste. Jesus threw the money changers out of the temple — and Judas was horrified! He was finally convinced he was getting nowhere with Jesus, except deeper and deeper into trouble.

(She paces back and forth again, in agitation; she gets out a handkerchief and blows her nose.)

37

Well — you all know what he did. Even I, his mother, can't find an easy way to say it — he sold Jesus to the Pharisees. For 30 miserable pieces of silver, he betrayed his gentle master. I don't know what he thought would happen to Jesus — perhaps he hadn't really thought about that part of it at all, because when he discovered that Jesus was to be crucified, Judas went crazy.

He stormed back into the high priest's house, and threw the 30 pieces of silver on the floor, screaming that he had betrayed innocent blood — and then he went and hanged himself. And it was all over. All over for Judas — all over for Jesus — but not all over for me.

(She spreads her hands wide in appeal to the audience.)

What could I have done? When he was a little boy, how could I have kept money from becoming his god? Even now, I don't know. But I keep going over and over it in my mind. I pray God will forgive me for having failed as a mother. I hope none of you will ever have to live with memories as black as mine. Thank you for listening.

(Exit.)

The Soldier's Story

Good Friday

(Enter LEADER, stage left)

LEADER: We are privileged tonight to have with us a Roman centurion named Cornelius, who is of special interest to us because he commanded the execution squad that crucified Jesus. Sir — if you would please come up on the stage —

(CORNELIUS, who is sitting in the front pew, gets to his feet slowly, looking around him uneasily. He is wearing a silver tunic, belted with a sword belt, and a short red cloak. He has sandals on his feet. Helmet is not necessary. He proceeds almost reluctantly up on the stage, stage right.)

LEADER: I am not exactly sure how to address you —

CORNELIUS: Just call me Cornelius. *(He is looking around the room.)*

LEADER: Very well, Cornelius. Does it make you uncomfortable to be here?

CORNELIUS: Not uncomfortable, exactly. It is certainly unfamiliar. It seems strange to find myself here. And the things you want me to talk about — well, I'm still trying to come to grips with some of them myself.

LEADER: I think I understand. Let's sit down.

(He indicates two chairs on stage, center front, about six feet apart. They sit, facing partly toward each other, but mostly toward the audience.)

Let's begin with something that doesn't make you uncomfortable. Tell us a little about the life of a Roman soldier.

CORNELIUS: *(sitting back in his chair and folding his arms)* My father was a soldier, and from the time I was a little boy, I never thought there was any other good choice for a man, except to serve Caesar.

All the world is Rome. And there is one master of it all, and that is Caesar. When a man becomes a Roman soldier, he becomes part of a very well organized system. Everywhere there is civil order and stability, and we centurions see that it stays that way.

But one cannot help seeing that having order and stability does not necessarily mean that there is justice. There is oppression for those who are not the friends of Caesar. The tax collector takes grain from the fields, and flax from the looms, to feed and clothe our legions, or to fill Caesar's hungry treasury. The impressor compels people for the arenas, for the cruel games that entertain the crowds. The executioner quiets those who raise their voices in protest. There is persecution of men who dare to think differently. Most of all, everywhere, there is contempt for human life. What is one man, more or less, in a crowded world?

40

LEADER: You were part of the system, and yet you saw this side of things?

CORNELIUS: I couldn't help seeing it. But for a long time, I tried not to think about it.

LEADER: Then what happened?

CORNELIUS: Then all of a sudden, there was a man, not a revolutionary, but a teacher, a healer, who raised his voice in Galilee. I was often sent to the places where he was, because he attracted huge crowds. My soldiers and I were crowd control, to remind the Jews that it would be unhealthy to create a riot. They are an emotional people.

LEADER: Were the crowds unruly?

CORNELIUS: Not usually. If they were lively, they quieted down when we appeared. And when the man Jesus began to speak, they were quiet as mice. Even out on the edges of the crowd, we soldiers could hear every word he said.

LEADER: And what did the voice from Galilee have to say?

CORNELIUS: He spoke of the sacredness of human life, of the value of every human soul, of the importance of each person reaching out in kindness to help others. He talked about a new kingdom in which each man can walk in dignity, and bow to none but his God.

LEADER: That doesn't sound like the kind of message Caesar would have welcomed.

CORNELIUS: We didn't report it. The man wasn't preaching revolution — at one point, he even told the people, "Render unto Caesar the things that are Caesar's, and unto God the things that are God's." I doubt if even Tiberius would have quarreled with that.

41

LEADER: So — how did you feel, when you discovered you had been given the task of crucifying this man Jesus, whom you admired?

CORNELIUS: You want the truth? I was sick inside. I'm a soldier — and I've seen my share of bloodshed on the battlefield. But we're Roman soldiers — not executioners. And the man Jesus was not an enemy, nor a criminal. He was a wise and gentle man. I'll admit it — I didn't want any part of it. But I was a soldier under orders — and we weren't given a choice.

(He gets up and walks back and forth behind the chairs.)

It must have been building up inside me for a long time, this thing about justice. I used to believe the Roman government was the best system there was. But it isn't just — not to people who aren't Roman citizens. I would like my life to stand for something — something I can be proud of. But if it doesn't stand for justice, what does it stand for?

(He comes back and sits down again.)

You can see why I'm struggling. It would be very tough for me to admit that my whole life has been given to defend something that isn't worth defending — that is rotten inside. That was what impressed me most about Jesus. He stood for something, and it was something good. And he believed in it enough to die for it.

The man died as nobly as he had lived. Crucifixion is an excruciating death, and its victims are usually screaming and cursing. But Jesus looked down at the soldiers and me, and asked his Father to forgive us for nailing him up there! I could have wept.

LEADER: You have been quoted as saying something very interesting at the crucifixion, at the moment when Jesus died. Would you like to tell us about that?

CORNELIUS: You mean, when I said, "Truly, this man was the Son of God!"? Yes, I meant it. He spoke to his Father several times, as he hung there dying — and as he died, his Father responded! There was a terrifying darkness, and a crashing of thunder as lightning split the sky. Now that was real! I went down on my knees beside the cross — for I believed then, and I believe now, that God is his father, and that everything Jesus said about himself was true. I count myself lucky that God didn't strike me dead for my part in the crucifixion.

LEADER: What will you do now, Cornelius?

(Cornelius stands up again)

CORNELIUS: I don't know. Being a soldier is the only trade I know. Perhaps the God who is the Father of Jesus can make some use of a centurion who wants to live the way Jesus lived. If he wants me, I am sure he will let me know.

Farewell.

(Exit CORNELIUS, stage right.)

LEADER: Farewell, Cornelius.

(Exit LEADER, stage left.)

Witness By Two Angels

Easter

(There are three seats on stage. Enter LEADER, stage left.)

LEADER: Welcome to everyone on this glorious Resurrection Day! We have a very special treat for you today. We are blessed to have with us as special guests the two angels who attended the tomb of Jesus on that first, long-ago Easter morning.

They have graciously agreed to appear like men, with their own brilliance concealed, in order to spare our eyesight, and to keep from terrifying us. Ladies and gentlemen — their heavenly excellencies, GABRIEL and MICHAEL!

(Enter with stateliness, stage right, GABRIEL and MICHAEL, dressed in white robes with long sleeves; no wings.)

GABRIEL: Lo! *(raising his arms)*

MICHAEL: Behold! *(raising his arms)*

(They stand side by side, calmly, with upraised arms. LEADER appears a little ill at ease.)

LEADER: Er — gentlemen, could we all relax a little, and perhaps sit down and talk informally? *(He gestures toward the chairs.)*

GABRIEL: *(to MICHAEL)* What do you suppose "informally" means?

MICHAEL: *(to GABRIEL)* He probably means "at ease." *(He lowers his arms.)*

GABRIEL: Oh. *(He lowers his arms.)* *(to the LEADER)* You must pardon us, but in our interactions with humankind, we seldom speak "informally," as you call it. We do pronouncements most of the time.

MICHAEL: Generally beginning with "Lo!"

GABRIEL: Or "Behold!"

LEADER: May I persuade you to sit down? If you remain standing, it is possible you might frighten some of the congregation.

MICHAEL: Of course. *(He sits.)*

GABRIEL: No problem. *(He sits. LEADER Also sits, obviously relieved.)*

LEADER: We would like to hear about your experiences at the tomb of Jesus on the first Easter morning.

MICHAEL: That was a magnificent assignment.

GABRIEL: It certainly was. The entire Host of Heaven had been in mourning while the Lamb of God was being tortured; but when the Lord Jesus shouted "It is finished!" and gave up his spirit, the rejoicing in heaven began. And the very first part of our assignment, Michael's and mine, was to rip the curtain outside the Holy of Holies in the temple from top to bottom.

MICHAEL: It was strange how Jesus' friends forgot that he had told them he would rise again in three days, and his enemies remembered it. The chief priests and the Pharisees went to Pilate and requested that a guard be placed at the sepulchre — to keep the disciples from stealing the body, they said.

GABRIEL: In simple truth, I think it was because they were afraid. Some of them had been present when Jesus called Lazarus forth from his tomb — and they feared Jesus might come forth from his own tomb!

MICHAEL: So they put a seal on the stone door of the sepulchre, and set a guard of soldiers to stand watch over the grave. It was an absurdly futile effort against the power of the Lord of Heaven and Earth.

LEADER: So then, what happened next?

GABRIEL: Michael and I waited until the small hours of the next morning, when the night was pitch black and cold. Then God the Father shook the ground, and we sailed in with a blaze of angelic splendor. Michael rolled away the stone from the mouth of the grave, and sat upon it. And all those poor soldiers, completely overcome with terror, fell unconscious to the ground.

LEADER: So you rolled away the stone so that Jesus could come out —

GABRIEL: Not at all! The Lord Jesus needed no one to open a door for him! He had already left the tomb when Michael rolled away the stone. No — it was rolled away to permit the women and the disciples to go in, so they could see that the tomb was empty.

LEADER: Oh, I see.

MICHAEL: The women came shortly before dawn. We could hear them talking to each other, wondering how they would be able to roll away the stone so that they could apply the spices they had brought to the Lord's body. I let Gabriel do the talking to the women. He's the messenger angel — he's good at that sort of thing.

GABRIEL: I had to begin by calming their fears, of course. Michael and I were in full angel dress, in honor of the occasion.

LEADER: What did you say?

GABRIEL: I told them we knew they were seeking Jesus; and that he was not here, because he had risen as he said he would. And I gave them the guided tour of the tomb, so they could see for themselves. Then I sent them away with the message that the Lord would go ahead of them to Galilee, where they would see him.

LEADER: Did they believe you?

MICHAEL: Oh yes! They went scampering away like frightened sparrows. Except one, and that was Mary Magdalene, who came a little later. She did not see Gabriel and me, and she thought someone had stolen the Lord's body.

LEADER: *(he consults his notes)* And wasn't she the one who told the disciples?

GABRIEL: Yes; and Peter and John ran at once to the tomb to investigate. We did not show ourselves to them — it was our orders.

MICHAEL: But Mary Magdalene saw the Lord Jesus himself, after John and Peter had left. It was a very tender meeting.

LEADER: Tell us what became of the soldiers.

MICHAEL: That was interesting, because it was a capital offense for a soldier to sleep while on guard duty — and here the entire squad had passed out. They went to the chief priests who had sent them, and reported what had happened. The priests took counsel and because they could not deal with the truth of the situation, instead of having the soldiers executed they bribed them to tell people that the disciples had stolen the body by night.

GABRIEL: Some of the Jewish people still believe that, although no one has bothered to explain how the disciples could have gotten past the armed guard.

LEADER: And is that the end of the story?

GABRIEL: It is the end of our part — but perhaps, it may be just the beginning, for those of you who may find yourselves for the first time among the believers this morning. We have told you the truth. Believing is up to you. *(Raising his arms as he stand up)* Lo! Got to keep in practice! And farewell!

MICHAEL: *(Also standing up, and raising his arms)* Behold! *(He and Gabriel lower their arms, and raise a hand in farewell to the LEADER; exeunt, stage right.)*

LEADER: Many thanks for coming! It was a privilege to have you! *(He waves in farewell as angels disappear down center aisle. Exit LEADER, stage left.)*